Internet Addiction
in Children
Causes, Help and Therapy
Luisa Ludwig

Introduction to the topic of online addiction in children

Advancing digitalization and the increasing availability of the Internet have changed our world and offer us many advantages and opportunities. The internet has become an important source of information and communication, especially for children and young people. However, there are also risks associated with the use of online media, such as online addiction. Online addiction, also known as internet addiction or computer game addiction, is a phenomenon that has been increasingly discussed in recent years. It refers to uncontrollable and compulsive behavior in dealing with online media, which can lead to negative consequences for the person affected and their environment. Children and young people are particularly affected by online addiction. At a time when the internet is playing an increasingly important role in young people's lives, children are often unprotected and unprepared for the dangers that the internet can bring. These include not only the excessive use of computer games, but also the intensive use of social networks, online shopping, video games or online gambling. There are many reasons why children and young people can become addicted online. These include the desire for recognition and popularity through social networks, escaping from problems in real life or simply the desire for distraction and entertainment. However, online addiction is often also a symptom of underlying problems such as depression, anxiety or attention disorders. The effects of online addiction can vary greatly. In children and young people, it can lead to a deterioration in school performance, social isolation, concentration problems, sleep disorders and physical complaints such as back pain and eye problems. Online addiction can also lead to psychological problems such as depression, anxiety and addiction. In order to prevent online addiction in children and young people, it is important that parents, teachers and educators inform themselves about the topic and raise awareness. Good education about the risks and consequences of online addiction and about a healthy approach to online media is essential. Parents should also make sure that children and young people have enough time for other activities and that they do not spend excessive amounts of time in front of screens. A balanced diet and sufficient exercise also help to reduce the risk of online addiction. However, if parents or other caregivers notice signs of online addiction in a child or young person, it is important to act quickly. In such cases, a conversation should be sought and professional help sought if necessary. For example, psychotherapists, family counseling centers or addiction counseling centers can be contacted.

What is online addiction and how does it develop?

Online addiction is a behavioural disorder characterized by the excessive use of online technologies such as social media, online games or online shopping. Those affected can no longer stop being online, even if this has a negative impact on their personal and social life. Online addiction is caused by a combination of biological, psychological and social factors. Here are some of the main causes: Biological factors: some studies have shown that people who are more prone to addictive behavior may have a genetic predisposition. In addition, research has shown that the reward system in the brain of people suffering from online addiction reacts similarly to that of drug addicts. Online addiction can also be triggered by psychological factors such as anxiety, depression or loneliness. People who have difficulty forming or maintaining relationships may also tend to engage in online communities and social media. Social factors: The constant availability of online technologies can lead to people spending more time online than they would actually like. Social media use can also cause people to constantly compare and pressure themselves, which can lead to an increased pattern of use. Symptoms of online addiction can vary, but typical signs can include: Loss of control: Those affected can no longer control the time they spend online and feel uncomfortable when they are not online. Withdrawal from social activities: People suffering from online addiction often neglect their friends, family and social activities in order to spend more time online. Problems at work or school: online addiction can cause people to have difficulty concentrating on their work or school and can affect their performance. Affected individuals may also develop physical symptoms such as sleep disorders, headaches or vision problems. Online addiction can have serious consequences. People who are addicted can destroy relationships, lose their job or get into financial difficulties. They can also develop a range of mental health problems such as anxiety, depression and social phobias. There are several treatment options for online addiction, which can vary depending on the severity of the condition and the individual's needs. Some possible options include cognitive behavioral therapy, family therapy, withdrawal therapy and medication.

Symptoms and signs of online addiction in children

Online addiction is a growing problem in children as more and more time is spent online and technology use becomes more integrated into everyday life. It is important to know the symptoms and signs of online addiction in children in order to intervene at an early stage. Change in mood: Children suffering from online addiction may show a change in mood if they cannot be online or if they have to limit their online activities. They may be irritable, sad or angry. Loss of interest in other activities: Children suffering from online addiction may lose interest in other activities they used to enjoy. They prefer to be online instead of meeting up with friends or playing sports. Problems at school: Children who spend too much time online may have difficulty concentrating on their schoolwork. They may get lower grades, neglect their homework or disrupt lessons. Sleep disorders: Children who suffer from online addiction may have difficulty falling asleep or sleeping through the night. They may be online late into the night, which can lead to fatigue and concentration problems during the day. Physical complaints: Children who spend too much time online may experience physical ailments such as headaches, back pain or eye problems. Changes in eating behavior: Children who suffer from online addiction may change their eating behavior. They may eat less or consume more unhealthy snacks while online. Secret online activities: Children suffering from online addiction may engage in secret online activities to deceive their parents or other adults. For example, they may hide their online time or interact with strangers in online chats. Neglecting personal hygiene: Children suffering from online addiction may neglect their personal hygiene. They may prefer to be online instead of washing themselves or taking care of their teeth. Changes in social behavior: Children suffering from online addiction may show changes in social behavior. They may withdraw from friends, stop participating in activities or engage in online communities instead of meeting in person. Loss of control: Children suffering from online addiction may have difficulty controlling their online use. They may not be able to disconnect from their devices or keep going back even though they know it is having a negative impact on their lives. It's important to note that online addiction can look different for each child. Some children may only show one or two symptoms, while others may have all of the symptoms listed.

The effects of online addiction on physical health

Online addiction, also known as internet addiction, is a growing problem in our digitalized world. The constant availability of internet connections and digital devices has led to an increasing dependence on internet use, which can have an impact on the mental health of those affected. This article takes a closer look at the effects of online addiction on mental health. First of all, online addiction can lead to a lack of social interaction. People who spend a lot of time online tend to spend less time with friends and family and instead focus on their online activities. This can lead to them feeling isolated and having a lower quality of life. Another problem with online addiction is that it can lead to sleep disturbances. If someone spends a lot of time being online, this can cause them to stay up late at night, disrupting their sleep cycle. This can lead to sleep disturbances, which can contribute to a deterioration in mental health. Online addiction can also cause affected individuals to neglect their responsibilities. If someone spends so much time online that they neglect their work or school, this can lead to problems at work and in their personal life. This can lead to anxiety, depression and low self-esteem. Another possible effect of online addiction on mental health is a deterioration in cognitive abilities. If someone is constantly online, this can lead to them having difficulty concentrating on a task or organizing their thoughts. This can lead to a deterioration in cognitive ability, which in turn can contribute to poorer mental health. Online addiction can also lead to an addiction to social media. If someone spends a lot of time using social media, this can lead to comparison thinking, which can lead to lower self-esteem and a deterioration in mental health. Furthermore, the constant use of social media can lead to individuals entering a bubble where they only receive information that confirms their own beliefs and opinions. This can lead to a loss of ability to understand and appreciate other perspectives. Online addiction can also lead to a loss of the ability to relax and unwind. If someone is constantly online, this can cause them to have difficulty relaxing and unwinding. This can lead to a deterioration in mental health, as rest and recovery are vital for good mental health.

The effects of online addiction on mental health

Online addiction, also known as internet dependency or internet addiction, is a growing problem in our modern world. The increase in online activities, including social media, online gaming and online shopping, has led to an increase in online addiction. This addiction can have a serious impact on mental health. In this article, I will explain the effects of online addiction on mental health in more detail. Isolation and loneliness Online addiction can cause those affected to isolate themselves from the outside world and become lonely. They spend their time surfing online instead of meeting up with friends or family. This can lead to a deterioration in mental health, as social contact is important to counteract depression and anxiety. Depression and anxiety Online addiction can lead to depression and anxiety. Constantly surfing the internet can make those affected feel depressed or anxious. It can also lead to sleep disorders and concentration problems. Depression and anxiety can worsen over time and lead to serious problems. Impairment of cognitive abilities Online addiction can also impair cognitive abilities. Constant use of the internet can make it difficult for those affected to concentrate on a task or retain information.

This can affect academic or professional performance and lead to a lack of success and self-esteem. Physical symptoms Online addiction can also cause physical symptoms such as neck and back pain, eye strain and headaches. Constant use of the computer or smartphone can lead to muscle tension and eye problems, which can have a negative impact on health. Loss of self-control Online addiction can cause those affected to lose control of their online activities. They spend more and more time online, even though they are aware that this has a negative impact on their health and life. The loss of self-control can lead to a vicious circle that is difficult to break. Addictive behavior Online addiction can also lead to addictive behavior. Sufferers feel the need to be online to feel better and may have withdrawal symptoms when they are not online. They may also lose interest in other activities they used to enjoy and their lives become all about their online activities. Online addiction in children can have many negative effects on their physical and mental health. It is important to recognize and diagnose this addiction early so that appropriate measures can be taken to support children.

How to recognize and diagnose online addiction in children

Online addiction in children often manifests itself through excessive playing of video games, excessive use of social media or online streaming services. Children suffering from online addiction cannot control their online activities and spend hours online. They neglect their schoolwork, hobbies and social relationships in order to spend more time in front of the screen. If children are prioritizing online activities over exciting real-world activities, this is a warning sign. It's important to watch for behavioral changes in children, especially if they suddenly become irritable or aggressive when they can't be online. Children suffering from online addiction may also have difficulty concentrating or have trouble falling asleep. These symptoms can also indicate other mental disorders such as depression or anxiety, so it is important that a specialist makes an accurate diagnosis. If parents suspect that their child is suffering from online addiction, they should first try to talk to their child about their concerns and address the issue sensitively and openly. It is also important to limit the number of hours the child spends online and ensure they get enough sleep and have a balanced diet. It can also be helpful to encourage real-world activities and engage the child in social activities to boost their self-esteem. If parental efforts to treat online addiction are not successful, they should seek professional help. A specialist doctor or psychologist can make a comprehensive diagnosis and create a treatment plan to support the child. This may include behavioral therapy, family therapy or medication, depending on the child's individual needs. In some cases, online addiction can also be caused by underlying mental disorders such as depression or anxiety. An accurate diagnosis is important to ensure the child receives the right treatment. Early diagnosis and treatment can help alleviate the symptoms of online addiction and put the child on the road to recovery. Overall, it is important to watch for behavioral changes in children and limit the number of hours they spend online. Parents should also try to encourage real world activities and itegrate the child in a social environment.

What parents need to know about online addiction

Internet use has become a necessity for children and teens today. However, with the increase in online activities, the possibility of online addiction has also increased. As parents, it is important to be aware of this danger and ensure that your children are surfing the internet safely and sensibly. Below you will find some important information about online addiction that can help you as parents to support your children in their use of the internet. What is online addiction? Online addiction refers to the excessive use of online activities such as social media, video games, online shopping or pornography. It is similar to other addictions such as alcohol or drug addiction. Online addiction can lead to a dependency where children and young people see the internet as their only source of pleasure and relaxation. How can you as a parent recognize online addiction? Online addiction can be difficult to recognize as children and teenagers usually try to hide their online activities. However, some signs of online addiction are: Changes in your child's mood and behavior. Decrease in hobbies and interests. Neglecting schoolwork and social obligations. Use of online activities as a means of coping with stress and problems. Sleep problems and changes in sleep patterns. Neglect of personal hygiene. How can you as a parent prevent online addiction? As parents, you can prevent online addiction by: Setting rules for internet use: Set rules for internet use together with your children and make sure they follow them. Setting limits: Limit the amount of time your children are allowed to spend online. Make sure that your child also has enough time for other activities. Be a role model: As parents, be a role model for healthy internet use. Encourage activities: Encourage other activities such as sports, hobbies and social activities. Monitor: Monitor your children's online activities and talk to them about what they are doing online. What can you do as a parent if your child is already addicted? If your child is already addicted, it is important to act quickly and seek professional help. See a doctor or therapist who has experience in treating online addiction. Early intervention can help your child overcome their addiction and recover from the negative effects of online addiction. Conclusion Online addiction is a serious matter and can lead to a variety of problems, especially for children and teenagers. As a parent, it is important to be aware of how the internet is affecting your children's lives.

How to prevent your child's online addiction as a parent

The internet has become an integral part of most people's lives. Even children and teenagers often use it as part of their everyday lives. However, there is a risk that they will become addicted to the internet and in particular to online games, social networks and videos. As a parent, it's important to prevent your child's online addiction and help them build a healthy relationship with the internet. Here are some tips on how you as a parent can prevent your child's online addiction: Set clear rules It is important to set clear rules for internet use. These include, for example, that the child may only use the internet at certain times, that certain websites or apps are blocked or that the child must not disclose any personal data on the internet. These rules should be drawn up together with the child and reviewed regularly. Time limits on the duration of use It is important to limit the duration of use to prevent the child from spending too much time online. The child's interests should be taken into account so that they do not feel unfairly treated. One option would be, for example, to allow the child to spend a certain amount of time online each day and to decide for themselves when they want to use this time. Use child-friendly content There are special child-friendly search engines and websites that offer child-friendly content. It is important that the child also finds such content on the Internet and does not only deal with content that is intended for adults. Parents can help by suggesting suitable content and, if necessary, supervising the child's Internet use. Shared use of the Internet Parents can use their child's interest in using the Internet to spend time together. Shared activities such as playing online games or watching videos can promote the child's understanding of how to use the internet properly. Shared use can also help to ensure that the child spends less time online alone and is therefore less at risk of getting lost in a virtual world. Have regular conversations Regular conversations with your child about their internet use are important in order to find out which sites they visit and what content they consume. In this way, parents can recognize whether the child is in danger of becoming addicted and take action in good time. Such conversations can also help to make the child aware of possible dangers on the internet and show them how to avoid them. Offer alternatives It is important to offer the child alternatives to Internet use. Joint leisure activities such as sports, arts and crafts or reading can help to ensure that the child does not spend too much time online and is therefore less at risk of becoming addicted.

How you as a parent can treat your child's online addiction

The modern world has revolutionized access to technology and the internet. The digital world offers a multitude of benefits and opportunities to make daily life easier. However, the internet and the use of digital devices can also become a serious problem, especially when it comes to online addiction. Many children and teenagers spend hours a day online, which can lead to an addiction that negatively impacts their health and daily life. In this article, we write about how parents can treat their child's online addiction. The first thing parents need to do is recognize that their child has an online addiction. If the child spends most of the day being online and their daily activities are affected, it's time to act. Create rules: Parents should set clear rules to limit the use of digital devices and internet browsing. For example, parents should set time limits for the use of digital devices and ensure that the child spends at least one hour a day in nature or playing with friends. Encourage interests: Parents should help their child find alternative interests that they enjoy and keep them from spending most of their time online. These include activities such as sports, music, art or crafts. Have conversations: Parents should talk to their child about the risks and dangers of the internet and teach them how to surf safely online. They should also teach them how to protect themselves online from cyberbullying and online scams. Shared activities: Parents should plan shared activities with their children to strengthen their bond and discourage them from being online all the time. This includes activities such as cooking, arts and crafts or game nights. No digital devices at the dinner table: Parents should ensure that no digital devices are allowed at the dinner table. They should encourage their children to focus on eating and socializing with the family. Technology-free time: Parents should ensure that their child does not use digital devices for at least one hour before bedtime. This helps to improve sleep and calm the brain. Seek professional help: If the problem is more severe and the child does not change despite the above measures, parents should seek professional help. There are therapists and counselling services that specialize in treating online addiction in children. Be a role model: Parents should be aware that they are role models for their children. If parents spend a lot of time online themselves, it will be difficult for children to adhere to these rules. Parents should therefore review their own behavior and limit their own internet use.

How teachers can recognize and treat their students online addiction

Technology has developed immensely in recent years and its use has become indispensable in most people's lives. However, students have the ability to transcend their technology addiction by immersing themselves in the online world. This addiction can have a negative impact on their mental and physical health as well as their academic performance. As a teacher, it is important to recognize the signs of online addiction in students and find ways to help them. First, teachers should understand that online addiction is a serious matter and that they cannot simply tell students to reduce or give up their technology. Teachers should also note that not all students who spend a lot of time online are addicted. The goal is to identify students who have problems caused by excessive online activity. To identify signs of online addiction, teachers should look for changes in behavior. Students who are addicted may lose interest in hobbies or activities they used to enjoy. They may also neglect sleep or withdraw to spend more time online. It is important to pay attention to how much time students spend online and whether it is affecting their academic performance. Students who are addicted may also be irritable or restless when they are offline. If teachers notice signs of online addiction in a student, they should take time to talk to them. Teachers should not rush to judgment or criticize students, but should try to understand the student's behavior and help them. Teachers should also reach out to students and ask them questions to help them understand their online activities and the impact they are having on their lives. Teachers should also provide students with alternative activities to help them spend their time offline. Teachers can encourage students to get involved in sports, music or other activities that can divert their attention from the online world. Teachers should also let parents know if they notice signs of online addiction in a student, as parents can help support the student. Teachers should also ensure that they teach students how to use the internet safely and responsibly. They should teach students how to protect themselves from cyberbullying, how to use social media responsibly and how to protect their online privacy. Helping students understand how to use the internet safely and responsibly can help make them less susceptible to online addiction. Overall, identifying and treating online addiction in students is a complex issue that requires a comprehensive approach.

Online addiction and social media

Online addiction and social media are a big issue these days More and more people are spending a large part of their day online and on social platforms such as Facebook, Twitter, Instagram, etc. This can have both positive and negative effects on their lives. On the one hand, social media enables people to network and share information and ideas. They can help people from different parts of the world to get in touch with each other and make friends. Important information and news can also be disseminated quickly, which can be particularly useful in crisis situations. On the other hand, however, the use of social media can also lead to addictive behavior. People can become addicted to the likes, comments and validation they receive on social platforms. This often leads to them spending more and more time on these platforms and isolating themselves from their real lives. Addiction to social media can also have a negative impact on mental health. It can lead to people constantly comparing themselves and putting pressure on themselves to keep up with others. This can lead to anxiety, depression and other mental health issues. Additionally, the use of social media can lead to a loss of privacy. Many platforms collect data about their users and use it for advertising or other purposes. This can lead to people feeling watched or tracked and feeling less safe to share their thoughts and information online. It is important to note that the use of social media is not bad per se. It depends on how much time you spend on these platforms and how you use them. It's important to find a healthy balance between online and offline time and to be aware of the impact social media use has on your life. There are various strategies to reduce or control social media use. One way is to make conscious decisions about how much time you spend on these platforms and what kind of content you consume. Another way is to unsubscribe from certain platforms or turn off notifications to be less distracted. It is also important to find alternative ways to connect and spend time with others. This can include meeting friends and family, pursuing hobbies or discovering new interests. By discovering new interests and activities, you can also make new friends and acquaintances that don't just happen online. Overall, it is important to understand the impact of social media use on your life and make conscious decisions about how you use these platforms.

Online addiction and video games

Online addiction and video games are two concepts that are closely linked. More and more people are spending a large part of their free time playing video games and becoming addicted to them. But what exactly is behind these terms and what effects do they have on the people affected? Online addiction is a relatively new form of addiction that has developed due to the increasing use of the internet. It is not just about the pure time spent in front of the computer or smartphone, but also about the way in which the internet is used. Online addiction can manifest itself in various forms, such as addiction to social networks, online shopping or video games. Video games have been a popular leisure activity for many years and offer a wide range of opportunities to immerse yourself in other worlds and experience adventures. However, due to increasing networking and online functionality, video games have become a real phenomenon that captivates many people. One of the main causes of online addiction in relation to video games is the fact that many games are becoming increasingly complex and time-consuming. In order to achieve certain goals or unlock achievements, players have to invest more and more time and often have to be online regularly. As a result, it can quickly happen that real life is neglected and players spend more and more time in front of the screen. Another cause of online addiction in connection with video games is the social component. Many games today offer the opportunity to interact online with other players and solve tasks together. On the one hand, this can be very motivating and fun, but on the other hand it can also lead to players investing more and more time in order not to disappoint their online friends or to climb up the rankings. The effects of online addiction in connection with video games can be manifold. On the one hand, it can lead to social isolation and neglect of friends and family. On the other hand, physical and psychological problems can also occur, such as back pain, eye problems, sleep disorders or depression. There are various approaches to preventing or treating online addiction in connection with video games. On the one hand, special therapies or counseling services can help you to reflect on your own behavior and make targeted changes. On the other hand, technical solutions, such as automatically switching off the computer after a certain period of time, can also help to control one's own behavior. Overall, it is important that the use of video games and other online services is conscious and reflective. Care should always be taken to ensure that real life is not neglected and that one's own health is not put at risk. This is the only way to limit the use of video games and other online services.

Online addiction and streaming services

Online addiction and streaming services are a widespread phenomenon these days. More and more people are spending a large part of their free time consuming streaming services such as Netflix, Amazon Prime Video or Disney+. This can lead to a dependency on the use of these services, which can have a negative impact on people's lives and social environment. Online addiction refers to the excessive use of online technologies, which can lead to an impairment of daily life. In 2018, the World Health Organization (WHO) recognized gaming disorders as a mental illness that can also be transferred to the use of streaming services. Excessive use of streaming services can lead to sleep disorders, loss of social contacts, isolation and neglect of other activities. One reason for the growing popularity of streaming services is that they offer a wide range of content at an affordable price. Users can choose from a wide range of films, series and documentaries and watch them anytime, anywhere. Another reason is that many users do not have the time to watch their favorite shows on TV due to work, family or other commitments. With streaming services, however, they can consume their favorite content in their free time. However, the consumption of streaming services can also lead to addiction. One of the causes of this addiction is the brain's reward system. When a person watches a series or movie they like, the brain releases dopamine, a hormone associated with pleasure and happiness. When the brain releases dopamine regularly, it can lead to a craving for more, which can lead to excessive consumption and neglect of other activities. Another cause of addiction to streaming services is availability. Since streaming services are available anytime, anywhere, it can be hard not to use them. It can be difficult to control yourself and stop yourself from using it, especially when it comes to exciting and engaging content. To prevent addiction to streaming services, there are several tips you can follow. First, set clear goals for how much time you want to spend streaming each day or week and stick to them. It's also important to find alternative activities that you enjoy doing and that don't conflict with streaming consumption, such as exercising or reading. A good work-life balance can also help to reduce the urge to stream excessively. Another tip is to focus on watching content that you really care about rather than getting lost in the endless choice of content.

Online addiction and online shopping

Online addiction and online shopping are two terms that are becoming increasingly present in today's digital world. The ability to buy anything from home has made shopping more convenient for many people, but it has also led to some people becoming addicted to online shopping and the internet in general. Online addiction is a form of behavioral addiction in which people exhibit excessive use of the internet that interferes with their work, social relationships, and life overall. There are different types of online addiction, such as online shopping addiction, online gaming addiction, social media addiction and pornography addiction. Online shopping addiction occurs when someone regularly and excessively stores online and feels like they are losing control. This addiction can lead to financial difficulties as sufferers often spend money they don't have to buy things they don't need. The causes of this addiction can be many, including loneliness, stress, boredom and lack of self-esteem. One way to avoid online addiction and online shopping addiction is to be aware of how much time you spend online and what activities you engage in. It is also important to be aware of how much money you spend on online shopping and how this affects your financial situation. If you find that you have problems controlling your use of the internet, it can be helpful to seek professional help. Another way to avoid online shopping addiction is to find alternative activities that can satisfy the need to store online. For example, you can try to get more involved in the real world by exercising, socializing with friends or volunteering. On the other hand, online shopping can also have positive effects. It can be a convenient way to buy things, especially if you don't have time to go to a store or if the product you want isn't available locally. It can also compare prices and choose the best deal, which in turn can lead to savings. Online shopping can also help people with mobility impairments or social anxiety to buy products without having to leave the house. Overall, online shopping is a convenient and practical way to buy things, but it's important to be aware of how much time and money you spend on it and how it affects your life overall. Online addiction and online shopping addiction can have serious consequences, but there are ways to avoid or overcome these problems. It is important to find a healthy balance in your use of the internet and online shopping and find alternative activities to lead a fulfilling life.

Online addiction and online dating

Online addiction and online dating are two closely related phenomena that have become increasingly important in recent years. The increasing digitalization of our society has led to more and more people maintaining their social contacts online and also increasingly looking for partners online. But while online dating is an opportunity for many people to find a partner for life, online addiction can quickly become a serious problem. Online addiction refers to the excessive and uncontrolled use of online services. Those affected often spend several hours a day on the internet, whether playing games, chatting or surfing. In doing so, they neglect their social contacts, their work or their studies and often lose track of time. The consequences can be serious: from social isolation and psychological problems to physical complaints such as eye problems or back pain. Online dating, on the other hand, is a way for many people to find a partner for life. Singles can use dating apps such as Tinder, Bumble or Lovoo to quickly and easily meet potential partners and arrange dates. Online dating offers many advantages: You can get to know each other at your leisure before meeting in real life, you have a wider choice of potential partners and you can also get in touch with people you might never have met in real life. However, online dating also carries some risks. For one thing, it can be difficult to find the right partner in the sea of profiles. Many people present themselves differently on their profiles than they actually are, which can lead to disappointment or even cheating. On the other hand, it can also be dangerous to meet strangers from the Internet. It is important to always be careful and meet in public places. For people who are prone to online addiction, online dating can quickly become an addiction. Constantly checking profiles and writing messages can have similar effects to playing computer games or surfing the internet. If those affected can no longer control themselves and their online activities are interfering with their lives, they should seek professional help. Overall, online addiction and online dating are not purely negative phenomena, but also offer opportunities and possibilities. However, it is important to consciously address these issues and be aware of your own online activities. If you deal with online dating in a conscious and controlled manner, you may well find a partner for life. However, if you notice that you are at risk of becoming addicted, you should seek professional help in good time.

Online addiction and cyberbullying

Online addiction and cyberbullying are two issues that are closely linked and are becoming increasingly important in today's world. The availability of internet access, smartphones and social media has led to an exponential increase in online activity. But while the internet offers a wealth of benefits, it also carries some serious risks. One of these is online addiction, where people become addicted to using the internet, gaming, social media or online shopping. Another threat is cyberbullying, which refers to the increase in attacks, harassment, humiliation or intimidation via the internet or social media. Online addiction, also known as internet dependency or internet addiction, is a serious problem that can affect the daily lives of those affected. There are various forms of online addiction, including computer game addiction, social media addiction, online shopping addiction, online pornography addiction and cyber relationship addiction. Sufferers often spend hours online, neglecting their work, social commitments and even their own health. They may experience physical symptoms such as insomnia, back pain, eye problems and headaches, as well as emotional discomfort, including anxiety, depression and irritability. The reasons for online addiction can be varied and often depend on the type of addiction. For example, computer gamers may become addicted to the feeling of being successful, while social media addicts may use their online identity for self-affirmation. Online shoppers may feel gratification from buying things, while porn addicts may seek excessive sexual gratification. Cyberrelationship addicts may seek relationships online and see them as a substitute for their real-life social interaction. Cyberbullying is a form of bullying that takes place online or via social media. It refers to intentional, repeated and harmful behaviors designed to humiliate, threaten, harass or embarrass someone. The perpetrators can be either known individuals or complete strangers. Unlike traditional bullying, the victim of cyberbullying can be targeted not only at school or work, but also at home or even in public. Cyberbullying can take various forms, including insults, rumors, threats, embarrassment, nude photos or videos, and unwanted contact. The effects of cyberbullying can be devastating for the victim, leaving them feeling isolated, depressed, anxious and helpless.

Online addiction and sexting

Online addiction and sexting are two issues that are becoming increasingly prevalent in today's digital world. Online addiction refers to the uncontrolled and compulsive use of online platforms, while sexting refers to the sending of sexually explicit messages or photos over the internet. In this text, we will discuss the impact of these phenomena on society and possible measures to prevent or manage them. Online addiction is a relatively new disorder characterized by a constant craving for attention, approval and social interaction. It can take various forms, such as excessive use of social media platforms, online games, pornography or online shopping. The reasons for the development of online addiction can vary greatly and range from personality traits such as self-confidence or social isolation to mental illnesses such as depression or anxiety disorders. The effects of online addiction on society are diverse and can have both individual and social consequences. The individual consequences include, for example, neglect of friends and family, sleep disorders, depression or anxiety. On a social level, online addiction can lead to a loss of productivity, as those affected spend less time working or studying and are more frequently absent due to illness. Online addiction can also lead to a distortion of reality, as those affected often only filter through the virtual world and neglect reality. Sexting, on the other hand, also has its own effects on society. While there are some positive aspects, such as increased sexual satisfaction and a closer bond between partners, there are also many negative consequences. One of the biggest dangers of sexting is the distribution of intimate images or videos without the consent of the people involved. This can lead to public exposure, bullying and in some cases even sexual abuse. The effects of sexting can also be felt on an individual level. Some people may suffer from anxiety, depression or suicidal thoughts after being a victim of sexting. There may also be an increased risk of becoming a victim of sextortion. Sextortion refers to the blackmailing of people who have shared intimate photos or videos in order to coerce further nudity or other acts. To avoid or manage online addiction and sexting, there are some measures that can be taken. One option is to limit or monitor the use of social media platforms and other online tools. It can also be helpful to take a break from the online world and focus on other activities.

Online addiction and pornography

Online addiction and pornography are two terms that are becoming increasingly common in today's digital world. The constant availability of the internet and smartphones makes it easy to be online anytime, anywhere and have access to countless content. But for some people, the behavior can become an addiction, especially when it comes to consuming pornography. Online addiction is defined as an uncontrolled behavior that is triggered by the use of the internet or other digital devices. This can manifest itself in various forms, such as gaming, social media addiction or online shopping. Pornography consumption can also lead to online addiction. One problem with consuming pornography is that there is an infinite amount of content and it is hard to stop. It can quickly become a compulsion to constantly search for new content and spend more and more time on it. This can lead to negative effects on life, such as lack of sleep, social isolation and problems in relationships. Another challenge associated with online addiction and pornography is the fact that it is often linked to feelings of shame. People suffering from pornography addiction often find it difficult to talk about it or seek help. They can feel isolated and lonely, which in turn can lead them to spend even more time online. There are also many health effects associated with online addiction and pornography use. Eye strain from staring at a screen for hours on end can lead to headaches, vision problems and fatigue. The lack of exercise and physical activity can lead to weight gain and other health problems. And the emotional strain of consuming pornography can lead to depression, anxiety and other mental health issues. If you think you may be suffering from an online addiction or pornography addiction, it's important to seek help. There are many resources available to you, from counseling services and support groups to therapies and medical treatments. It is important to realize that you are not alone and that there are many people struggling with similar issues. There are also steps you can take to reduce your online addiction and use of pornography. Here are some tips: Set fixed times when you are allowed to be online and stick to them. Avoid consuming pornography and other unhealthy content. Spend more time with real people and activities. Try to focus on your goals and interests instead of getting distracted by the online world.

How to make the internet safer as a parent

The internet has had a significant impact on our society and daily lives in recent years. For children in particular, the internet is a great way to access knowledge and information, stay in touch with friends and entertain themselves. At the same time, however, the internet also carries some risks, especially for children who are moving in an increasingly digital world. As a parent, it is important that you are aware of how you can make the internet safer for your children. Here are five ways you can make the internet safer for your children: Monitor your children's online activity: it is important that you know what kind of websites your children are visiting and who they are communicating with online. Therefore, monitor your children's online activities and talk to them about which websites and activities are safe and which should be avoided. Install parental control software: There are many different types of parental control software that can help you make the internet safer. For example, this software can restrict access to certain websites or apps or send you alerts if your children are viewing inappropriate content or communicating with strangers. Talk to your children about online safety: It's important that you talk to your children about online safety. Explain to them what types of information they should share online and what should be avoided. Also talk to them about cyberbullying and what they should do if they are confronted with it. Set rules for internet use: Set rules for internet use, such as how much time your children are allowed to spend online and when they are allowed to use the internet. Make sure that your children understand these rules and that they understand the consequences if they don't follow them. Encourage your children to tell you about their online experiences: Encourage your children to tell you about their online experiences, especially if they feel uncomfortable or are being bullied by others. Make sure your children know that they can trust you and that you will help them if they need help. In summary, the internet has many benefits but also some risks, especially for children. As a parent, it is important that you are aware of how you can make the internet safer for your children. Monitor your children's online activity, install parental control software, talk to your children about online safety, set rules for internet use and encourage your children to tell you about their online experiences. By taking these steps, you can make the internet safer for your children and help them to enjoy the benefits of the internet without being exposed to the risks.

How to make the internet safer as a teacher

As a teacher, internet safety plays an important role in imparting knowledge and promoting learning. With the rise of cybercrime, online harassment and the spread of misinformation online, it's important that teachers teach their students how to act safely and responsibly online. Here are some ways teachers can help make the internet safer: Teach cybersecurity and digital ethics lessons: teachers should hold regular cybersecurity and digital ethics lessons to educate their students about the risks of online threats such as viruses, malware, phishing and identity theft. It is also important to inform them about what they can do to protect their personal information and devices. In addition, teachers should teach students how to use digital resources responsibly, such as dealing with copyrights, online plagiarism and the spread of misinformation. Installing security software: Teachers can help their students to install and regularly update security software on their devices. This software protects against viruses, malware and other online threats. In addition, teachers can ensure that their schools and classrooms are equipped with a firewall and other protective measures to prevent access to inappropriate or dangerous websites. Encourage the use of strong passwords: Teachers can encourage students to use strong passwords that consist of a combination of letters, numbers and symbols. In addition, students should be instructed to change their passwords regularly and not to use passwords for different accounts. Teachers can also educate on the importance of two-factor authentication to increase account protection. Monitoring online activity: Teachers should regularly monitor their students' online activity to ensure they are adhering to school policies and not engaging in inappropriate or dangerous activities online. It is important that teachers inform their students that their activities online are being monitored and that they maintain a trusting and open relationship with them. Encourage open communication: Teachers should encourage students to ask questions and raise concerns about their online safety and digital privacy. Open communication between teachers and students can help students feel safer and more comfortable using the internet.

How to make the internet safer as a child protector

The internet is an incredible resource for children, but there are also numerous risks and dangers they may encounter on this medium. As child protectors, there are many things we can do to make the internet safer and protect children from potential dangers. Below are some tips and recommendations: Educate parents and guardians: One of the most important things we can do to make the internet safer is to educate parents and guardians about what dangers may be lurking online. They should be educated about the different types of online threats, such as cyberbullying, online pornography, fraud and identity theft. Create child-friendly online environments: There are many child-friendly online environments designed specifically for children to provide them with a safe and educational online experience. As child protection advocates, we should work to ensure that these child-friendly platforms are further developed and improved. Use safe search engines: Children use search engines to find information and explore the internet. We should therefore ensure that they use child-friendly and safe search engines that do not display inappropriate content. Encourage parent-child communication: It is important that parents and children talk openly about children's online activities. Parents should encourage their children to ask questions and help them make online decisions. Teach children how to use social media safely: Social media is one of the main sources of online threats. As child protectors, we should teach children how to use social media safely and protect themselves from cyberbullying and other threats. Teach children that they should not share personal information online: Children should learn that it is dangerous to share personal information online. As child protectors, we should teach them what information they should not share, such as their name, address and date of birth. Teach children how to recognize online scams and phishing attacks: Children should learn how to recognize online scams and phishing attacks to protect themselves from these threats. This includes teaching them to ignore suspicious emails and messages and not to click on unknown links. Encourage parents and guardians to use technology: There are many technologies that can help make the internet safer for children, such as parental control software and filters. As child protection professionals, we should encourage parents and guardians to use such technologies to protect their children online.

The government's role in tackling online addiction in children

In today's digital world, online addiction among children and young people has increased at an alarming rate. In response, governments around the world need to take action to address this challenge and ensure the safety and wellbeing of children. One of the most important roles of government is to provide education and awareness. It is important that the government informs the public about the effects of online addiction and emphasizes the importance of healthy online behavior. This can take the form of campaigns, public service announcements or training for teachers and parents. Governments can also introduce special programs in schools that inform children and young people about the risks of online addiction and help them to develop healthy behavior. Another important aspect is cooperation with online service providers. Governments can put pressure on companies to ensure that they offer safer products and services and limit the use of addictive behavior. Some countries have already passed laws to ensure the protection of children and young people online. For example, the UK government has introduced an Age Appropriate Design Code, which ensures that online services are safe and age-appropriate by default. The government can also promote initiatives that help children and young people to control and reduce their online use. An example of this is the introduction of time limits for the use of online services or the promotion of offline activities. Governments can also encourage the development of technologies that help parents and teachers to monitor and control children's online activities. In addition, the provision of support and treatment for those affected is an important aspect. Governments can provide resources to support the research and development of treatments and therapies for online addiction. They can also set up specialized clinics and facilities to receive and treat those affected. Finally, collaboration between government, communities and families is essential. The government can encourage collaboration between schools, families and communities to ensure that everyone is working together to tackle the problem of online addiction in children. For example, schools can work closely with parents to ensure that students' online use is monitored and controlled at home. Overall, the government's role in tackling online addiction in children is crucial. It requires a comprehensive strategy to organize measures to educate, work with providers, introduce control mechanisms, provide support and cooperation between municipalities and cities.

The role of schools in combating online addiction among children

The rapid growth of technology and online platforms has led to an increased risk of online addiction among children. Online addiction can manifest itself in various forms, including excessive use of social media, gaming, online shopping and other activities. Schools play an important role in tackling online addiction in children as they have a huge impact on children's lives and have the opportunity to educate them about the risks of online addiction and take preventative measures. One of the most important roles schools play in tackling online addiction is to educate children about the risks and effects of excessive online use. Schools can take a number of measures to inform students about the effects of online addiction, such as information sessions, seminars or workshops. It is important that students understand the negative effects of online addiction in order to protect themselves from it and to be better able to seek help if they find themselves in this situation. Another important role that schools play in tackling online addiction is to take preventative measures. Schools can take steps to ensure that students do not go online excessively, for example by restricting the use of laptops, tablets and smartphones or blocking the use of certain websites. It is also important that schools inform students' parents so that they can also take steps to protect their children. Schools can also help to provide students with alternative activities to discourage them from going online excessively. Students should be encouraged to participate in various activities, such as sports, music, art and other recreational activities that promote their physical and mental health and help them improve their self-esteem and social skills. Schools can also offer special programs and workshops to teach students alternative skills that can help them be more productive and use their free time wisely. In addition, schools can also work with parents and other educational institutions to develop a joint strategy to combat online addiction. This can be achieved by organizing workshops, seminars or information events where parents and teachers are informed about the risks of online addiction and strategies for prevention and intervention are discussed. Overall, schools play an important role in combating online addiction in children by educating students about the risks, taking preventative measures, promoting alternative activities and cooperating with other educational institutions.

The role of parents in combating online addiction in children

In today's digital world, where technology is an integral part of our daily lives, children are often heavily exposed to the influence of the internet. Although the internet offers many benefits, it can also lead to an addiction known as online addiction. Online addiction can lead to a number of negative effects on children's lives, including impaired physical health, reduced academic performance and social isolation. Parents have a crucial role to play in preventing and combating online addiction in children. In this article, we will explore the different ways parents can help their children develop a healthy relationship with the internet. Raising awareness Parents need to be aware that their children are at high risk of becoming online addicts. As such, parents should be aware of what kind of online activities their children are engaging in and how long they are engaging in these activities. Parents should also be aware of the symptoms of online addiction, including physical and emotional symptoms such as back pain, sleep disturbances and irritability. Setting boundaries One of the most important ways parents can help their children develop a healthy relationship with the internet is to set boundaries. Parents should set a limit on the amount of time their children can spend online. They should also set specific times when their children are not allowed to be online, such as during mealtimes or before bedtime. This will ensure that children have time for other activities, such as outdoor games or social interactions. Be a role model Parents should set a good example for their children when it comes to using technology. They should reflect on their own behavior and make sure they don't spend too much time online. Parents should also ensure that they involve their children in family activities rather than spending their time online. Communication Communication is an essential part of any healthy relationship. Parents should talk to their children about the internet and make sure they feel comfortable asking questions or raising concerns. Parents should also talk to their children about how to use the internet safely, including using safety software and avoiding online interactions with strangers. Alternative activities Parents should encourage alternative activities to ensure their children are not spending too much time online. Children should be involved in activities that promote their physical and mental health, such as sports, art and music. Parents should also ensure that their children have enough time to interact with friends and family.

The role of therapists in the treatment of online addiction in children

Online addiction in children is a growing problem that can affect their physical and mental health as well as their academic performance and social skills. Early detection and treatment of online addiction is therefore crucial to help children find a healthy balance between online and offline activities. The role of therapists in the treatment of online addiction in children is very important as they have specialized skills and techniques to help children overcome their online addiction. First of all, therapists can help parents recognize online addiction in their children. Many parents may not be aware that their child has a problem with online addiction, as they may not know how much time their child spends online or what kind of activities they engage in. Therapists can help parents recognize the signs of online addiction, such as a decline in academic performance, social isolation, sleep disturbances and behavioral changes. Once online addiction is recognized, therapists can help children control their online activities. This can be achieved through various techniques such as setting time limits on the use of electronic devices, creating a schedule for offline activities and encouraging children to engage in social activities. Therapists can also use techniques such as mindfulness and relaxation exercises to help children reduce the stress and anxiety that often accompany online addiction. Another important role of therapists in treating online addiction in children is to help them build healthy relationships. Online addiction can cause children to lose social skills and isolate themselves. Therapists can help children learn new social skills to build healthy relationships. They can also involve family members to support the family and create an environment that promotes the child's recovery. In addition, therapists can also help identify the underlying emotional issues that may be causing children to develop online addiction. Stress, anxiety and depression can cause children to escape online. Therapists can help children identify these issues and give them the necessary tools and techniques to cope. Additionally, therapists can also provide therapy with the entire family. This can help improve the family's understanding and support of the child. Family members can also learn how to help the child develop healthy habits and overcome their online addiction.

The role of support groups in the treatment of online addiction in children

The use of online technologies such as smartphones, tablets and computers is widespread among children and adolescents. While the use of technology offers many benefits, it can also lead to overuse and online addiction. Online addiction is defined as a behavioral addiction in which those affected use online technologies in an uncontrolled and compulsive manner, leading to impairment in other areas of life. Online addiction in children is a growing problem as children and young people are particularly vulnerable to the effects of technology. Support groups can play an important role in the treatment of online addiction in children. In this article, we will take a closer look at the role of support groups in the treatment of online addiction in children. Support groups offer children and young people affected by online addiction the opportunity to meet with other sufferers and talk about their experiences. The groups provide a supportive and safe environment where children and young people can share their experiences and learn from others. Participants can benefit from the experience and knowledge of others to help them overcome their own problems. In self-help groups for online addiction in children, participants can learn how to control their technology use and organize their free time in a meaningful way. The groups also provide a platform for sharing strategies to avoid addictive behavior and develop healthy habits. Participants can learn from each other how to deal effectively with stress and how to find a balance between technology use and other activities. Online addiction support groups for children can also help participants develop social skills and improve their social relationships. Children and young people affected by online addiction often spend a lot of time isolated in front of screens and have difficulty developing social skills. In support groups, they can learn how to build and maintain relationships and how to communicate effectively. Another benefit of online addiction support groups for children is that they give participants a sense of belonging. Children and young people affected by online addiction often feel isolated and alone with their problem. In self-help groups, they can meet like-minded people who have had similar experiences. The groups offer a sense of community and cohesion, which can be important for recovery. Support groups for online addiction in children also provide support and resources for parents and caregivers. Parents and caregivers of children affected by online addiction can get advice and support from other parents and caregivers in support groups.

The future of online addiction in children

Online addiction in children is a serious problem that has been on the rise in recent years. Technology has dramatically changed the way we live, work and communicate, and children are often the ones most affected. In this article, we will look at the future of online addiction in children and what can be done to tackle this problem. Online addiction in children can manifest itself in different ways. Some children may spend hours in front of a screen playing games or browsing social media, while others may consume online pornography or other inappropriate content. In many cases, online addiction can lead to a reduction in social interaction and problems at school or at home. The future of online addiction in children depends heavily on the development of technology. More and more children have access to smartphones, tablets and computers, making it easier to go online and stay online for hours at a time. The increasing prevalence of virtual reality technology could also lead to new forms of online addiction in children, as children could become immersed in virtual worlds and neglect their real lives. To combat online addiction in children, parents, educators and society as a whole need to work together. Parents should educate their children about the risks of online addiction and set limits on how much time they can spend online. Educators should talk about online addiction at school and teach students how to stay safe online. Society should also take steps to limit access to inappropriate content and ensure that children are safe online. One way to combat online addiction in children is to promote alternative activities. Children should be encouraged to play sports, play with friends and spend time outside instead of sitting in front of a screen for hours on end. Parents should also ensure that children get enough sleep, as a lack of sleep can lead to an increased susceptibility to online addiction. Another important step to combat online addiction in children is to use technology responsibly. Children should be taught how to use technology safely and responsibly, rather than simply surfing for hours on end. Parents should also make sure they follow the same rules and set a good example for their children. Overall, online addiction in children is a serious problem that is likely to increase in the future. However, there are steps that can be taken to tackle this problem. Parents, educators and society as a whole need to work together to ensure that children use technology safely and responsibly and encourage alternative activities to limit the amount of time they spend online.

How to make better use of your time online as a child

The internet is an incredibly valuable resource for children, but it can also be very easy to get lost in it and waste valuable time. However, there are many ways that children can make better use of their time online and get the most out of their online activities. Learning and education: One of the main ways that children can make better use of their time online is through learning and education. There are a variety of online resources designed specifically for children, including learning programs, video courses and online libraries. Children can also watch YouTube videos to learn about a particular topic. It is important that parents monitor their children's online activity and ensure they are on sites that are appropriate for their age. Creativity and hobbies: The internet offers many opportunities for children to develop their creative skills and pursue their hobbies. Children can write blogs, create videos, make music and publish artwork. There are also many online platforms that specialize in promoting creative activities for children, such as digital painting or photo editing. Parents can encourage their children to share their creative skills online and network with other children who have similar interests. Social interaction: The internet also offers many opportunities for children to interact with other children and develop their social skills. There are numerous online games that children can play and communicate with other children. Children can also use online chats and forums to talk to other children and exchange opinions. However, it is important that children are educated by their parents about the dangers of online interactions and that they never share personal information online. Internet safety: Internet safety is of utmost importance for children. It is important that parents educate their children about which online activities are safe and which are not. Children should be informed that they should never share their personal information online and that they should stay away from any online activity that makes them feel uncomfortable or that they do not understand. Parents should also make sure they monitor their children's online activity and alert them if they see anything suspicious or dangerous. Set boundaries: It is important that children keep their online activities within reasonable limits and that they do not waste their time online. Parents should set clear boundaries for their children about how much time they can spend online and what types of activities they are allowed to do. Parents should also make sure that their children have enough time for other activities, such as sports or social interactions outside of the internet.

How to improve your online social interactions as a child

In today's digital world, it is often easier for children to make friends online than in real life. If children learn how to improve their online socializing, it can strengthen their ability to connect and communicate in the real world. Use safe social networks: Using safe social networks such as Facebook for Kids, Kuddle or Kidzworld is a good place to start. These platforms are designed to create a safe and friendly environment for children to connect and interact with others. Be kind and polite: Children should always be kind and polite when interacting with others online. This means that they should not respond to negative comments or bullying, but instead send positive and supportive messages. Be authentic: Children should show themselves as they are online. They should not try to be someone else or put on a front. Instead, they should show their true personality to find others who have similar interests and hobbies. Find common interests: Children should try to connect with other children who have similar interests. For example, if they enjoy playing soccer, they can join an online soccer group and meet like-minded people. Be active: Children should actively participate in group or chat discussions and engage in conversations. They should also ask questions and ask others for their opinions. This will help them build connections with others and improve their social skills. Join online groups: Children should join online groups that focus on their interests and hobbies. These groups can be forums, chats or online communities. They can help children meet other like-minded people and make friends. Be careful with personal information: Children should be careful when sharing personal information online. They should not share personal information such as their address, phone number or school. They should also be careful when meeting up with someone they have met online. Have clear boundaries: Children should set clear boundaries when it comes to their online activities. You should set a certain amount of time per day or week that they are allowed to spend online. They should also know when it's time to go offline and focus on other activities. Use emojis and stickers: Children can use emojis and stickers to express their emotions and thoughts online. These can help to avoid misunderstandings and create a positive and friendly mood in online conversations. Connect online and offline activities: Children should try to connect their online and offline activities. How children can improve their learning and working habits online The internet offers a wealth of opportunities for children to improve their study and work habits. Here are some tips that can help: Structure your time: it's important that children use their time effectively to complete their tasks. One way to do this is to create a schedule of when they will do which tasks. They should also schedule breaks to relax and replenish their energy reserves. Use online resources: The internet is full of resources that can help children improve their study and work habits. From online encyclopedias and learning programs to apps and games, there are a variety of tools that make learning and collaborating with other children easier. Stay organized: Children should make sure they keep their assignments and notes organized. One way to do this is to create digital folders and notes on their computer or tablet. This way, they can easily find their work and have everything they need in one place. Use social media: Social media can also help children improve their study and work habits. There are groups and communities where they can discuss, ask questions and work on projects together with other children. However, it is important to make sure that they use social media safely and responsibly. Take breaks: Children should take regular breaks to relax and replenish their energy reserves. They should get up, move around and eat or drink something. One way to do this is to set an alarm clock to remind them to take a break. Get involved in online courses: Online courses are a great way for children to learn new skills and expand their knowledge. There are many online courses aimed at children that can help them discover and develop their interests and skills. Set goals for yourself: It is important that children set clear goals that they want to achieve. They should be realistic and achievable within a reasonable time frame. When children achieve their goals, they feel motivated and successful. Use online collaboration tools: There are many online tools that can help children collaborate with others. For example, they can use Google Drive to collaborate on documents or Skype to connect with other children and work on a project. Seek feedback: Children should seek feedback to learn how they can improve their study and work habits. They should seek feedback from teachers, parents, or other trusted individuals to learn what they are doing well.

How to monitor your child's online behavior as a parent

The internet is a great resource for children, but it can also be a dangerous one. As a parent, it's important to monitor your child's online behavior to make sure they are safe and not doing inappropriate things. Here are some ways you can monitor your child's behavior online: Use parental control software: There are many programs and apps that are called parental control software. You can install this software on your children's computers, laptops, tablets and smartphones to make sure they can only access age-appropriate content. Monitor your child's activity on social networks: Many children use social networks such as Facebook, Instagram and Snapchat to keep in touch with friends. As a parent, you should ensure that your child is not sharing or receiving inappropriate content. Monitor your child's activity on these sites and be aware of who their friends are. Check the browser history: Regularly check the browser history of your child's computer or cell phone. This will allow you to see which websites they have visited. If you discover inappropriate websites, you can talk to your child about them and explain why they should not access them. Set rules for internet use: Set clear rules for internet use, e.g. which websites your child is allowed to visit and how long they are allowed to be online. Talk to your child about the reasons for these rules and explain that they will help them stay safe. Talk to your child regularly about their online behavior: Talk to your child regularly about their experiences online and what they have learned. Explain to them how they should behave if they come across inappropriate content or cyberbullying. Be alert: Be alert to changes in your child's behavior. If they withdraw or feel uncomfortable, this could be a sign that they are being harassed or bullied online. Be a good role model: Be a good role model for your child. If you use the internet responsibly yourself, your child will be more likely to do the same. It is important to note that monitoring your child's online behavior should not mean that you distrust or want to control them. Rather, it's about making sure they are safe and not doing inappropriate things. It's also important that you talk to your child about why you are monitoring their online activity. Explain to them that you are concerned about their safety and that you want to help them use the internet responsibly.

How to limit your child's online behavior as a parent

In today's digital world, children often spend hours online. They use the internet for social media, games and to communicate with friends and family. But as parents, it's our responsibility to make sure they're safe and that they don't spend too much time on it. Here are some tips on how to limit your child's online behavior as a parent. Set clear rules: The first thing you should do is set clear rules for your child's internet use. You should set clear times when your child is allowed to use the internet and for how long. You should also define which websites and apps your child can and cannot visit. It is important that your child understands the rules and sticks to them. Monitor internet use: You should monitor your child's internet use. There are many software programs that can help you do this. These programs can give you an overview of which websites your child visits and how much time they spend on the internet. This way you can make sure that your child is following the rules. Talk to your child: It is important to talk to your child about the risks of the internet. You should inform your child that there are many dangers on the internet, such as cyberbullying, sexting and inappropriate content. You should also talk about how to stay safe online, how to protect personal information and how to deal with online harassment. Use parental control tools: There are many parental control tools that can help you limit your child's internet use. You can set up filters to block access to certain websites, and you can set up time limits to make sure your child doesn't spend too much time online. You should also make sure that the settings are applied to all of your child's devices, including smartphones and tablets. Use shared computers: If you have a shared computer, you should make sure that you set up a separate user account for your child. This way you can ensure that your child can only access certain websites and that they cannot access your private files. Keep track of your child's online activities. You should regularly check your child's online activity. Take a look at the websites they have visited and the apps they have downloaded. If you notice that your child is not following the rules or is behaving inappropriately online, you should talk to them about it and explain the consequences. Spend time online together: Spend time on the internet together with your child. In this way, you can teach them how to behave safely online. You can teach your child how to write e-mails, how to carry out online searches.

How teachers can monitor their students' online behavior

As a teacher, you have a responsibility for your students' behavior, not only in the classroom, but also online. The online world holds many dangers and potential distractions that can interfere with student learning. That's why it's important as a teacher to monitor student behavior online. Here are some ways this can be done: Internet filters Internet filters are programs that can restrict or block access to certain websites or online content. These programs can be used in school to ensure that students only access websites that are relevant to the lesson and not websites that are inappropriate or dangerous. Internet filters can also be set to block access to social media platforms such as Facebook, Twitter or Instagram. Monitoring emails Students often use email to communicate with teachers and classmates. It is therefore important that teachers monitor students' emails to ensure that they do not contain inappropriate or offensive content. This can be achieved by teachers having access to students' email accounts or by monitoring emails sent to students' school email address. Monitoring online chats Students may also communicate with each other via online chats, including platforms such as Skype or Google Hangouts. These chats can be monitored by teachers to ensure that students are not talking to each other inappropriately or becoming distracted. Teachers can also ask students to only chat online during certain times or for specific tasks. Use of monitoring software. Software that is able to monitor student behavior online. For example, this software can track students' keystrokes to ensure that they are only used for school-related purposes, or monitor the websites visited to ensure that students are not accessing inappropriate or dangerous websites. However, the use of monitoring software should be transparent, accountable and respectful of student privacy. Educating students Another way to monitor students' online behavior is to teach them how to use the Internet properly. Teachers can inform students about the dangers of the internet and teach them how to behave safely online. This includes how to critically evaluate online content and how to use social media responsibly. Overall, it is important that teachers monitor their students' behavior online to ensure that they are behaving safely and productively.

How teachers can limit their students' behavior online

The internet has taken on an increasingly important role in the lives of students and teachers in recent years. It offers many benefits and opportunities, but also some challenges. One of the biggest challenges is controlling and limiting student behavior online. Here are some tips on how teachers can limit their students' behavior online: Create school rules for the Internet: Teachers should create a clear school policy that governs student behavior online. These school rules should set out the school's expectations for student behavior online, including social media use, email use, and online safety. Explain the importance of privacy: Students should be informed about how to protect their privacy. They should be made aware of the risks of personal data online and the use of passwords. Use filters: It is important that schools have filtering on their internet connections to restrict students' access to certain websites and content. There are various filtering programs that can be used by schools to block inappropriate content. Monitor student activity: It is important that teachers monitor student activity on the internet to ensure they are complying with school rules. There are various tools that can be used by schools to monitor student activity online. Encourage positive online behavior: Teachers should encourage students to be positive online. Students should be taught how to communicate respectfully online, how to evaluate sources with confidence and how to browse the internet safely and responsibly. Create special learning modules: Teachers can also create special learning modules to make students aware of the dangers of the Internet and teach them how to keep their online activities safe and responsible. Communicate with parents: Teachers should also communicate with students' parents and let them know how they can help their children stay safe online. Use the help of experts: There are many experts who can help schools implement measures to restrict students' behavior online. Teachers should work with these experts to ensure that their students are acting safely and responsibly online. Overall, it is important that teachers restrict their students' behavior online to ensure that they act safely and responsibly online. By teachers creating clear school policies, using filters.

How to monitor children's behavior online as a child protector

As a child safeguarding professional, it is important to monitor children's behavior online to ensure their safety and wellbeing. The internet offers children many opportunities, but also many dangers. It is therefore necessary for adults, especially parents, teachers and educators, to pay attention to how children use the internet. One way to monitor children's behavior on the Internet is to use monitoring software. This software can be installed on a computer or mobile device and monitor the child's activities. It can record the websites visited, the time the child spends online and even the messages typed. This software can provide parents or caregivers with reports on the child's behavior online. Another way to monitor children's behavior online is to set up parental controls. These features are available on many devices and operating systems and can be configured to restrict access to certain websites or applications. Parents can also set time limits to ensure that children are not online for too long. It is also important that parents talk to their children about the internet and teach them how to use it safely and responsibly. Parents should explain to their children the dangers of the internet, such as cyberbullying, online scams and the spread of harmful content. They should also explain the importance of privacy and protecting personal data. To monitor children's online behavior, parents should also keep an eye on their online activities. They should be aware of what their children are doing online and who they are communicating with. Parents should ensure that they monitor their children when they use social networks or other online communities. Parents should also be aware of what their children are downloading and installing. Many apps and games may contain harmful content or put the child's privacy at risk. Parents should make sure they review the apps and games their children download and ensure they are safe and age-appropriate. In addition to monitoring children's behavior online, parents should also ensure that they have an open and trusting relationship with their children. Children should feel safe to talk to their parents about their online activities and ask for help if they encounter a problem. Finally, it is important to emphasize that the aim of monitoring children's behavior online is not to undermine the trust between parents and children. It's about ensuring the safety and wellbeing of children and making sure they use the internet safely and responsibly. Parents should work with their children to ensure they are aware of how to use the internet safely.

How to limit children's behavior online as a child protector

In today's digital world, children are increasingly online and interacting with others via the internet. Although the internet offers many benefits, it also comes with some risks. It is important that children are safe online and are aware of how they should behave online. As child protectors, there are several ways to limit children's behavior online and ensure their safety. Set clear rules: It's important that children have clear rules about how they should behave online. Work with your children to create rules for internet use, such as which websites they can visit, who they can communicate with online and what information they should disclose on the internet. Explain the consequences if the rules are not followed. Use filters: There is special filter software that restricts access to inappropriate content. This software can help you control internet access for your children and protect them from inappropriate content. Monitor internet use: Keep an eye on your children's internet use by checking their browsing history and monitoring the websites they visit. If you notice your child viewing inappropriate content or communicating with strangers online, talk to them about it. Talk to your children: It's important that you talk to your children about the risks of the internet and teach them how to stay safe. Explain to them that they should never give out personal information and that they should contact adults if they feel unsafe. Check social network settings: If your children use social networks, make sure their profiles are set to private and that they only accept friends they know personally. Also regularly check their friends list and remove people they don't know. Use parental control apps: There are many parental control apps that parents can use to monitor and restrict their children's online activities. For example, these apps can block access to certain websites or apps or set a schedule for internet use. Encourage offline activities: Encourage offline activities such as reading, sports or art to limit the amount of time your children spend online. This can help them find a better balance between online and offline activities. Be a role model: Be a good role model and show your children how to behave safely online. Avoid sharing private information online and talk to your children about your own experiences and challenges when using the internet.

Therapy for internet addiction

Internet addiction is a widespread problem that can manifest itself in various forms, such as obsessive use of social media, online gaming or pornography. It can lead to a loss of time, energy and social relationships and affect mental health. There are different approaches to internet addiction therapy that can be used depending on the individual case. Below are some of the options: Self-control: the person affected can try to gain control over their use of the internet themselves by setting certain rules and boundaries. This can mean setting yourself time limits or restricting certain activities. Therapy: Professional therapy can help to identify and treat the underlying causes of internet addiction. Various techniques such as cognitive behavioral therapy, mindfulness training or family therapy can be used in therapy. Group therapy: Group therapy can help to exchange ideas with other affected people and learn from their experiences. It can also help you feel less isolated and find social support. Medication: In some cases, medication may be prescribed to treat symptoms such as anxiety or depression associated with internet addiction. Behavior modification: Behavior modification focuses on changing unwanted behaviors through positive reinforcement. This can mean rewarding yourself for following certain rules or achieving goals. Technology Withdrawal: A radical solution may involve switching off from technology for a period of time. This can help to interrupt the behavior and reduce the dependency. Mindfulness:

Mindfulness can help to calm the mind and improve concentration. It can also help to become aware of why you use the internet so much and what emotional needs you are fulfilling. Support groups: There are various online and offline support groups where affected individuals can support each other and share their experiences. Sport and exercise: Sport and exercise can help to reduce stress and boost self-confidence. It can also help to reduce the need to sit in front of the computer for hours on end. Self-reflection: Regular self-reflection can help you become aware of the impact your internet use is having on your life and what changes you want to make. It can also help you to redefine your own values and priorities.

Imprint

Luna Ludwig
Am Anger 3
06869 Coswig
Germany
Luna-Publishing.de